Vegetarian Slow Cooker Recipe Book: 30 Easy Set It & Forget It Meals

By Maria Holmes

Table of Contents

Preface

Dear Reader!

I would like to take this opportunity to thank you for taking the time to read my book and hope that you find these vegetarian slow cooker recipes interesting and tasty!

Before we start our journey in the world of vegetarian slow cooker meals, I would like to introduce myself. My name is Maria Holmes and I am indeed the author of this vegetarian slow cooker recipe book that you are now reading. If you are interested in learning more about me, my mission and my passion, please join my Facebook community at *Homes Cooked Meals* for interesting activities and enthusiastic discussions. Or you might want to visit my blog at www.holmescookedmeals.com.

But let's get back to the topic at hand - *Vegetarian Slow Cooker Recipe Book: 30 Easy Set It & Forget It Meals*. The recipes you are about to see were born out of my passion for cooking simple and tasty vegetarian meals. This book consists of a collection of some of my favorite vegetarian slow cooker recipes for soups, beans, chilies, potatoes, rice, and desserts. They are easy to prepare, are good for you, and are also delicious and tasty.

If you are like me, you probably enjoy having dinner ready and waiting for you after your long day at work. These vegetarian slow cooker recipes will allow you to get a jump start on dinner in the morning without much effort. Plus, you will come home to the enticing aroma of a home-cooked vegetarian meal. Best of all, you can relax – dinner just about makes itself!

Your slow cooker is not only for the work-a-day world, but also for carefree entertaining. Slow cookers are ideal for serving a hot beverage, warming a dip, or on the buffet table because it keeps food hot and tasty for several hours.

Your slow cooker is the perfect partner when you're on the go, too. Whether it's a scout's banquet, a party at work, or a neighbor's potluck — you'll have no problem packing up your dish and keeping it hot.

So get ready to discover all the tasty simmered-in flavors of vegetarian slow cooking.

Enjoy and be well!

Maria Holmes

Acknowledgments

My family suggested that I write this vegetarian slow cooker recipe book a few months ago. While the idea was intriguing, I was also very terrified at the idea of writing a book. After all, I am a working mom and I have never written a book in my entire life.

But my family kept insisting that I compile some of my favorite recipes and share them with others. So I took the plunge and decide to author my first cookbook. And now that I have completed my first cookbook, I can't wait to share more of my recipes with the world.

Thank you, my caring and loving family, for recommending and encouraging me to share these mouth-watering recipes. Thank you, Mother Nature, for providing us with all the incredible ingredients that go into making these tasty meals. Thank you, technology, for inventing and perfecting the slow cookers and crock pots that allow us to make these great meals while freeing up our time to spend with our loved ones.

And most importantly, thank you, dear reader, for purchasing *Vegetarian Slow Cooker Recipe Book: 30 Easy Set It & Forget It Meals.*

Introduction

In today's busy world, things just seem to be getting faster, including the time we spend preparing meals. What a surprise to discover that using a slow cooker is an answer to every day dinner. Slow cooking is the best way to keep pace with our busy lives since the meal you're making requires little to no attention while it cooks, and you'll enjoy a home-cooked, good-for-you meal.

Vegetarians have quickly recognized the benefits of slow cooking. Preparing tasty vegetarian meals in a slow cooker allows all the veggies and seasonings the opportunity to fully release all their flavors, resulting in a more flavorful dish.

And you will also realize that the slow cooker's versatility does not stop there. As you will see in this book, you can use your slow cooker to make big batches of veggie chili, soups, rice, and even deserts.

Things to Consider

The end-result and success of any slow-cooker recipe depends largely on the capacity of your cooker and the total cooking time.

Based on my personal experience, I find that a slow cooker performs better when it is between half and two-third full. If you put too much food inside your slow cooker, you risk having the content sputter over or under-cooking your meal. If you don't put enough food into your slow cooker, you run the risk of burning your meal.

Similarly, if the cooking time is too short, you will have firm, bland and undercooked food, while over-cooking your food will burn, blackened or pulverize it.

Adapting Your Favorite Recipes

Don't be afraid to experiment with your slow cooker. Although it's not recommended that you remove the lid while cooking with a slow cooker, it may be a good idea to check your meal midway through the first few times you use it. This will help you avoid over-cooking your meals or breaking down the texture too much.

Another benefit of using a slow cooker is that you can adapt your favorite recipe without having to hunt for a new recipe! Using the following guidelines to help, you can adapt many of your favorite slow-cooker recipes.

Begin by finding a similar recipe in this cookbook. It will serve as a guide for quantities, amount of liquid and cooking time. Next, unless you're making a soup, decrease the amount of liquid in your recipe to about half because liquids does not boil away. For soups, simply leave the liquid level as recommended.

I have found that the flavor of dried basil strengthens during long cooking. If adapting a recipe using dried basil, I suggest that you cut the amount called for in half or add fresh basil during the last 30 minutes of cooking time.

Dairy products, such as milk, sour cream and cheese break down during long cooking times, and the sauce will curdled. Instead of using fresh milk, try canned condensed soups, non-fat dry milk powder or canned evaporated milk for a smooth, creamy sauce. For best results, add cream, sour cream or cheese during the last 30 minutes of cooking time or just before serving to prevent them from breaking down.

Finally, be sure to allow sufficient cooking time. Most soups, stews and one-dish meals require 8 to 10 hours on the low heat setting.

Choosing the Right Vegetarian Recipes

The key to making great vegetarian meals in the slow cooker is to select recipes hearty enough to endure several hours in the slow cooker.

Since vegetarian meals don't contain meat, they don't naturally make their own juices as they stew. So you should focus on dishes that contain some sort of cooking liquid, such as soups or stews. Avoid dry ingredients since these can burn in the slow cooker.

You should also look at recipes that incorporate plant-based proteins. However, many plant-based proteins break down or become mushy if left in the slow cooker for several hours. I would recommend that you stick to beans and lentils in slow cooker dishes. You should avoid quinoa, since it can't stand-up to the long cooking time.

Adding the Ingredients

Little "secrets", or tips and tricks, often make a recipe come out just right! From a picture-perfect appearance to the delicious vegetables, these success tips help to ensure each slow cooked meal comes with a healthy dose of praise.

So first thing first, always spray the inside of the slow cooker with cooking spray for easy clean-up.

Cooking tasty vegetarian meals in the slow cooker does require some preparation time. You will need to cut up all of your vegetables the night before and soak dried beans and lentils in water for at least eight hours before you put them in the slow cooker. That way, everything will be ready to load into the slow cooker the next day.

You also need to consider the order in which you add your ingredients if you want to prepare a successful meal.

When cooking vegetables in a slow cooker, you should always brown or roast any slow cooking vegetables that are typically blander in taste, such as potatoes, carrots, parsnips and squash. Place these vegetables into the slow cooker first, adding water, juice or broth to prevent burning and aid in the release of flavors. You should also add other longer cooking ingredients, such as beans, lentils and cut-up root vegetables first.

You can then add the other vegetables that soften more quickly, such as mushrooms, tomatoes or greens about 45 minutes before it's time to serve the meal. Always thaw frozen vegetables or rinse them with warm water to separate before placing them in the slow cooker. Adding frozen vegetables will lower the internal temperature, and the dish will take longer to cook.

Last but not least, you should add spices, seasonings and herbs near the end (typically during the last hour of cooking). Use dried leaf herbs instead of ground because they keep flavor during the long cooking time. Always taste before serving to see whether additional seasoning is needed.

Concentrate the flavor of juices in the slow cooker by removing the lid and cooking on the high heat setting during the last 20 to 30 minutes.

To create a more pronounced flavor in soups and stews, substitute broth for the water or add bouillon cubes with the water.

Ground red pepper (cayenne) and red pepper sauce tend to strengthen and become bitter during long slow cooking. Use small amounts and taste during the last hour of cooking and decide whether more seasoning is needed.

Beans, Beans!

Cooking dried beans in a slow cooker can be tricky because of the variations in electrical power and the types of minerals found in your local water. Beans need sufficient heat to tenderize them; dried beans cooked on the low heat setting for 8 to 10 hours may not be tender. I have found three ways to cook dried beans, and you can select the one that best fits your schedule. The most convenient way to cook a dried bean recipe is to put all the ingredients into the slow cooker and cook on the high heat setting until the beans are tender. I use this method for most of my dried bean recipes.

Another method is to cook the beans 2 to 3 hours on the high heat setting, and then reduce to the low heat setting for 8 to 10 hours. This is a little less convenient because you have to be available after a couple of hours to reduce the heat setting.

A more traditional method for cooking dried beans is to first place the beans and water in the slow cooker. Cover and cook on the high heat setting 2 hours. Turn off the cooker, and let the beans stand 8 to 24 hours. Change the water. Add the remaining ingredients, and cook on the low heat setting 8 to 12 hours or until done.

Soups

<u>THE RECIPES</u>

Veggie Packed Minestrone Soup

Cooking time: 6 to 8 hours (LOW), plus 20 to 30 minutes (HIGH)
Serves 6

Minestrone soup is a hugely popular vegetable soup that is very healthy and low in fat. This vegetarian slow cooker minestrone soup recipe has no oil, making it virtually fat free and low in calories. This is a good soup that lends itself to variations. You can experiment by adding extra veggies, such as sweet corn (one of my favorites!), green peas or even some chickpeas or white kidney beans.

Ingredients

4 cups vegetable broth
4 cups diced tomatoes
1 tablespoon fresh basil, finely chopped
1/2 teaspoon oregano
3 carrots, chopped
3 celery stalks, chopped
1/2 onion, chopped
2 zucchini, chopped
2 yellow crookneck squash, chopped
1 cup green beans, chopped
3 garlic cloves, minced
2 bay leaves
Salt and pepper to taste
1-1/2 cups macaroni pasta

Preparation

Combine all the ingredients except the pasta in a slow cooker.

Cook on LOW for 6 to 8 hours.

Add the pasta and cook on HIGH for 20 to 30 minutes (or until pasta is done cooking).

Remove bay leaves before serving.

<u>Nutritional Information (per serving)</u>

Calories: 168; Total Fat: 1.8g; Cholesterol: 0mg; Sodium: 558mg;
Carbohydrates: 30.5g; Dietary Fiber: 5.2g; Protein: 9.3g

Split Pea Soup

Cooking time: 4 hours (LOW)
Serves 8

Split pea soup typically uses ham for added flavor. But this vegetarian (and vegan) split pea soup gets its flavor by packing in spices like thyme, sage and bay leaves for a lower fat and cholesterol free version of the classic split pea soup.

Ingredients

2 cups green split peas
8 cups water or vegetable broth
3 vegetarian bouillon cubes*
2 potatoes, chopped
2 ribs celery, chopped (optional)
2 carrots, sliced
1 onion, diced
2 cloves garlic, minced
1 teaspoon dry mustard
1 teaspoon cumin
1 teaspoon sage
1 teaspoon thyme
3 bay leaves
Salt and pepper to taste

* Note that this will make the dish more salty … so use at your own discretion.

Preparation

Combine all the ingredients in the slow cooker.

Cover and cook on LOW for at least 4 hours, or until the peas are soft.

Remove the bay leaves before serving.

Nutritional Information (per serving)

Calories: 224; Total Fat: 1.0g; Cholesterol: 0mg; Sodium: 59mg; Carbohydrates: 41.8g; Dietary Fiber: 14.7g; Protein: 13.7g

Lentil Soup

Cooking time: 8 to 10 hours (MEDIUM)
Serves 6

This is an extremely easy vegetarian soup to make - just put all the ingredients in your slow-cooker in the morning and forget about it until the end of the day. This lentil soup is hearty enough to be a main dish in its own right, but you can always add extra veggies to make it even more filling. If you find the soup to be too bland, you can add fresh ground pepper. Other great suggestions would be 1/2 teaspoon cumin, 1/2 teaspoon garlic powder and one Bay leaf. But these are only optional!

Ingredients

2 cups lentils
4 cups water (for soaking the lentils only)
4 cups vegetable broth
1 onion, diced
3 stalks celery, sliced
2 carrots, chopped
2 cloves garlic, minced
1 teaspoon salt
1/4 teaspoon black pepper
1/2 teaspoon oregano
1 can (14 ounces) diced tomatoes

Preparation

Pre-soak the lentils in water for at least 2 hours (for better results, pre-soak the lentils overnight).

Drain the lentils and stir with all the ingredients into a slow cooker.

Cook on MEDIUM for 8 to 10 hours.

Enjoy your crock-pot lentil soup!

Nutritional Information (per serving)

Calories: 309; Total Fat: 2.7g; Cholesterol: 0mg; Sodium: 1,439mg;
Carbohydrates: 46.7g; Dietary Fiber: 21.4g; Protein: 24.1g

Cream of Mushroom Soup

Cooking time: 6 to 8 hours (LOW), plus 30 minutes (HIGH)
Serves 4

This cream of mushroom soup recipe is slow cooked for hours to really let the flavors mingle. Soy milk and vegan margarine make for a creamy base and mushrooms simmered in vegetable broth add plenty of flavors in this vegetarian (and vegan) slow cooker soup recipe.

Ingredients

1-1/2 cups sliced mushrooms
1/2 onion, diced
2 cloves garlic, minced
1 tablespoon margarine
3 cups vegetable broth
2 tablespoons flour
1 cup sour cream
1 cup milk or soy milk
Salt and pepper to taste

Preparation

Sautee the mushrooms, onion and garlic in the vegan margarine for 3 to 5 minutes, or until the onions turn soft.

Put the mushrooms, onions and garlic in a slow cooker and add the vegetable broth.

Cover and cook on LOW for 6 to 8 hours.

Add the remaining ingredients and cook on HIGH for another 30 minutes, or until the soup thickens.

Add more salt and pepper to taste.

Nutritional Information (per serving)

Calories: 235; Total Fat: 17.3g; Cholesterol: 30mg; Sodium: 664mg;
Carbohydrates: 11.7g; Dietary Fiber: 0.6g; Protein: 9.0g

Tomato Pesto Soup

Cooking time: 7 to 8 hours (LOW), plus 10 to 15 minutes (LOW)
Serves 6

Adding the instant rice at the end of the cooking time is a great trick which will work with almost any slow cooker soup or stew recipe.

Ingredients

1 onion, chopped
3 cloves garlic, minced
3 carrots, shredded
1 green bell pepper, chopped
1 can (14 ounces) diced tomatoes, undrained
1 can (6 ounces) tomato paste
1 teaspoon dried oregano leaves
1/2 teaspoon dried basil leaves
1/4 teaspoon pepper
1/2 teaspoon salt
2 cups water
2 cups vegetable broth or chicken stock
1 cup long grain brown rice
1/2 cup pesto
1/2 cup grated Parmesan cheese

Preparation

Combine all the ingredients, except for the rice, pesto and cheese, in a 3 to 4 quart slow cooker and mix to blend.

Cover and cook on LOW for 7 to 8 hours.

Stir in the rice, then cover and cook for an additional 10 to 15 minutes, or until the rice is tender.

In a small bowl, combine the pesto and cheese and blend. Serve with the soup.

Nutritional Information (per serving)

Calories: 320; Total Fat: 12.7g; Cholesterol: 12mg; Sodium: 897mg;
Carbohydrates: 41.4g; Dietary Fiber: 5.4g; Protein: 11.8g

Beans

THE RECIPES

Vegetarian Baked Beans

Cooking time: 8 to 10 hours (LOW)
Serves 10

Vegetarian Baked Beans is the perfect side dish for all occasions, from a family barbecue or picnic to a formal lunch or dinner with friends. Beans are an excellent source of protein for vegetarians, and this vegetarian slow cooker recipe is a cinch to make.

If you have a sweet tooth or are cooking for kids, you may want to try the vegetarian baked beans with pineapple recipe.

Ingredients

1 pound pinto or kidney beans
1 onion, diced
2 teaspoons white vinegar
1/2 teaspoon salt
1/3 cup brown sugar
1 can (6 ounces) tomato paste
4 tablespoons ketchup
1/4 cup margarine

Preparation

Cover the beans with water and soak overnight (add only enough water to cover the beans).

Add all the ingredients, including the soaking water, to a slow cooker and stir to combine.

Cook on LOW for 8 to 10 hours.

Nutritional Information (per serving)

Calories: 394; Total Fat: 8.6g; Cholesterol: 0mg; Sodium: 434mg;
Carbohydrates: 63.9g; Dietary Fiber: 13g; Protein: 18.7g

Sweet Pineapple Baked Beans

Cooking time: 6 to 8 hours (LOW)
Serves 8

This vegetarian slow cooker baked bean with pineapple recipe is a sweet side dish or light entrée that even the kids will love. It is easy and quick to prepare in your slow cooker and is great for a potluck or weekend lunch meal.

If you prefer to try something simpler without pineapple, then you should check out the Vegetarian Baked Beans recipe.

Ingredients

2 cans (19 ounces, each) pinto beans
1 can (8 ounces) pineapple chunks, drained
1 onion, diced
2 cloves garlic, minced
1/2 cup barbecue sauce
2 tablespoons maple syrup
1 tablespoon soy sauce
Salt and pepper to taste

Preparation

Cover the beans with water and soak overnight (add only enough water to cover the beans).

Mix together all the ingredients in the slow cooker.

Cover and cook on LOW for 6 to 8 hours.

Nutritional Information (per serving)

Calories: 143; Total Fat: 0.5g; Cholesterol: 0mg; Sodium: 1,074mg; Carbohydrates: 28.7g; Dietary Fiber: 5.2g; Protein: 5.2g

Refried Beans

Cooking time: 8 hours (MEDIUM-HIGH)
Serves 6

This slow cooker refried beans recipe is vegetarian, vegan and gluten-free. It is slow-cooked with jalapenos and spices, and then mashed.

Homemade refried beans are great low-fat side dish, and can be served with Mexican rice, or wrapped up into a burrito.

Ingredients

3 cups dry pinto beans
8-1/2 cups water
1 onion, diced
1/2 jalapeno pepper, seeds removed and minced
3 cloves garlic, minced
1/2 teaspoon cumin
2 teaspoons salt
1/2 teaspoon black pepper

Preparation

Cover the beans with the water and soak overnight.

Combine all the ingredients, including the soaking water, in a slow cooker and stir to combine.

Cover and cook on MEDIUM-HIGH for 8 hours.

Drain out most of the water.

Mash the beans with a potato masher, adding back in some of the liquid if needed.

Nutritional Information (per serving)

Calories: 346; Total Fat: 1.3g; Cholesterol: 0mg; Sodium: 798mg;
Carbohydrates: 62.8g; Dietary Fiber: 15.4g; Protein: 21.0g

Sweetened Vegetarian Baked Beans

Cooking time: 6 to 8 hours (LOW)
Serves 8

Expecting a large group of people? Then vegetarian baked beans are an excellent choice. It is simple and inexpensive to make a large batch of baked beans, especially slow cooker baked beans. And vegetarian baked beans are low in fat, cholesterol-free and high in fiber and protein!

Ingredients

1 pound navy beans or Great Northern beans
Water (enough to soak the beans)
1/2 cup molasses
3 tablespoons ketchup
1 teaspoon mustard powder
1 cup brown sugar
1 tablespoon vegetable broth powder
1/2 teaspoon salt
Dash black pepper, or to taste

Preparation

Soak the bean in water in a large covered soup or stock pot.

Bring the water to a slow simmer. Cover and cook for 30 to 45 minutes, or until the beans are barely soft.

Drain the water from the beans, but keep the water for later.

Whisk together the molasses with the remaining ingredients in a small bowl.

Combine the beans, molasses, ketchup, mustard powder, brown sugar, vegetable broth, salt, pepper, and the cooking water from the beans in the slow cooker.

Cover, and cook on LOW setting for 6 to 8 hours, or until the beans are soft.

Enjoy your vegetarian baked beans!

Nutritional Information (per serving)

Calories: 331; Total Fat: 1.0g; Cholesterol: 0mg; Sodium: 306mg; Carbohydrates: 70.1g; Dietary Fiber: 13.9g; Protein: 13.0g

Three Bean Cassoulet

Cooking time: 30 minutes (HIGH), plus 8 to 9 hours (LOW), plus 1 hour (LOW)
Serves 6

This meatless low fat main dish is full of hearty beans and vegetables.

Ingredients

1 cup dried lima beans
1 cup dried great Northern beans
1 cup dried garbanzo beans
4-1/2 cups water
16 ounce bag baby carrots
1 onion, chopped
3 garlic cloves, minced
1 tablespoon dried parsley flakes
1 teaspoon dried basil leaves
1/2 teaspoon dried thyme leaves
1/2 teaspoon salt
1/8 teaspoon white pepper
1 bay leaf
1 can (14 ounces) diced tomatoes, undrained
2 tablespoons tomato paste

Preparation

Cover the beans with cold water in a large saucepan and bring to a boil.

Let boil for 1 minute, remove from heat, cover, and let sit for 1 hour.

Drain the beans and combine the beans, 4-1/2 cups water, carrots, onion, garlic and seasonings except salt, tomatoes, and tomato paste in 3-1/2 to 4 quart slow cooker.

Mix well, cover and cook on HIGH for 30 minutes.

Reduce heat to LOW and cook for 8 to 9 hours or until the beans and vegetables are tender.

Stir in the tomatoes, tomato paste, and salt, cover, and cook 1 hour longer on LOW.

Remove the bay leaf before serving.

Nutritional Information (per serving)

Calories: 310; Total Fat: 2.8g; Cholesterol: 0mg; Sodium: 419mg; Carbohydrates: 57.5g; Dietary Fiber: 17.2g; Protein: 16.5g

Chilies

<u>THE RECIPES</u>

Vegetarian Chili

Cooking time: 6 to 8 hours (LOW)
Serves 8

Making vegetarian chili in a slow cooker is the same as cooking up a batch on a stove-top. The only difference is that you need to add a little bit more liquid. And like any other chili, you should adjust the seasonings to taste and add extra veggies (if you prefer).

This is a plain meatless slow cooker chili recipe for vegetarians and vegans. It's low-fat, cholesterol-free, and high in fiber and protein.

Ingredients

2 tablespoons oil
4 cloves garlic, minced
1 onion, chopped
1/3 teaspoon red pepper flakes
1 teaspoon oregano
1 can (28 ounces) tomatoes
1 tablespoon soy sauce
1 tablespoon chili powder
1/3 teaspoon cumin
1-1/2 cups vegetable broth
1 can (6 ounces) tomato paste
2 cans (19 ounces, each) black beans, drained
2 cans (19 ounces, each) red kidney beans, drained

Preparation

Sautee the onion, garlic and red pepper flakes until the onion is soft (about 3 to 5 minutes).

Add the chili powder and cumin and cook for two additional minutes.

Place the onions and the remaining ingredients in the slow cooker, stirring to combine.

Cover and cook on LOW for 6 to 8 hours.

Nutritional Information (per serving)

Calories: 321; Total Fat: 5.3g; Cholesterol: 0mg; Sodium: 887mg;
Carbohydrates: 50.3g; Dietary Fiber: 18.3g; Protein: 20.0g

Very Veggie Chili

Cooking time: 6 to 8 hours (LOW)
Serves 5

This slow cooker vegetable chili recipe doesn't skimp on the veggies or the flavor. All you need to do is put all the ingredients in your slow cooker and come home to a healthy and complete vegetarian meal after a long day at work.

Although this recipe is very tasty if you follow the instructions exactly, it is the perfect platform for all you "recipe experimentalist". If you find it a little bland, then just add some extra clove of garlic, a dash of salt, a heaping of paprika or some oregano. That will spice it up!

Ingredients

1 onion, diced
2 cloves garlic, minced
1 red or yellow bell pepper, chopped
2 carrots, grated or sliced thin
1-1/2 cup corn
1 zucchini, diced
2 cans (19 ounces, each) kidney beans
2 cans (15 ounces, each) diced tomatoes
1/2 cup water
1-1/2 tablespoon chili powder
1 teaspoon cumin
1/2 teaspoon red pepper flakes
Dash cayenne pepper
Dash Tabasco sauce (optional)

Preparation

Combine all the ingredients in a slow cooker.

Cover and cook on LOW for 6 to 8 hours.

Nutritional Information (per serving)

Calories: 264; Total Fat: 2.3g; Cholesterol: 0mg; Sodium: 356mg;
Carbohydrates: 51.8g; Dietary Fiber: 13.7g; Protein: 14.2g

Vegetarian Barley Chili

Cooking time: 6 to 8 hours (MEDIUM-LOW)
Serves 6

This is a super easy to prepare vegetarian chili recipe made with healthy barley and beans. Just dump everything into your slow cooker and a few hours later you'll have a delicious and nutritious high-protein vegetarian chili.

Ingredients

1 onion, diced
4 cloves garlic, minced
2 cans (19 ounces, each) kidney beans
3/4 cup pearled barley
1 can (15 ounces) diced tomatoes
2 tablespoons chili powder
1/4 teaspoon cayenne pepper
3 cups water
Salt and pepper to taste

Preparation

Combine all the ingredients in a slow cooker.

Cover and cook on MEDIUM-LOW for 6 to 8 hours.

Add more salt and pepper, to taste.

Nutritional Information (per serving)

Calories: 288; Total Fat: 2.3g; Cholesterol: 0mg; Sodium: 684mg; Carbohydrates: 54.2g; Dietary Fiber: 14.4g; Protein: 13.6g

Roasted Tomato and Corn Chili

Cooking time: 3 to 4 hour (HIGH) or 3 to 8 hours (LOW)
Serves 4

Not only is this chili roasty-toasty, delicious and spicy, but it's also amazingly healthy and easy to make. Simply chop some vegetables and roast them in the oven in olive oil and chili powder. Then mix the roasted veggies with a few cans of this and that in the slow cooker and walk away for a few hours or even all day. Voila!

Ingredients

1 can (14 ounces) Mexican style diced tomatoes
1 large onion, chopped
1 large bell pepper, chopped
1-1/2 cups frozen corn, thawed
1 tablespoon minced garlic
2 tablespoons olive oil
2 to 4 tablespoons chili powder
1 teaspoon cumin
1 minced hot pepper, such as Serrano (if desired)
2 cans (14 ounces, each) undrained beans, any variety such as pinto,
black, or kidney, undrained
1 cup vegetable broth or V8

Preparation

Drain the tomatoes, pouring the juices directly into the slow cooker.

Preheat the oven to 425°F. Line a cookie sheet with foil and place the tomatoes, onion, bell pepper, corn and garlic on the cookie sheet. Drizzle with olive oil and sprinkle with chili powder and salt and pepper to taste.

Roast in the oven until the vegetables are softened and speckled with brown, stirring occasionally, about 30 minutes.

Combine the vegetables and remaining ingredients into the slow cooker.

Cook on HIGH for 3 to 4 hours or on LOW for 6 to 8 hours.

Taste for seasoning before serving. Add salt, pepper, or more chili powder if needed.

Serve with sour cream and green onions if desired.

<u>Nutritional Information (per serving)</u>

Calories: 290; Total Fat: 9.2g; Cholesterol: 0mg; Sodium: 1,652mg; Carbohydrates: 41.4g; Dietary Fiber: 11.5g; Protein: 11.4g

Chili with Sweet Potatoes

Cooking time: 7 to 8 hours (LOW) or 4 to 5 hours (HIGH)
Serves 5

This one is simple, cheap and delicious. My one word of caution is that it may be too spicy for some. If you find it too hot to handle, try adding a can of tomato sauce to dilute it out. You can also try to add 1/2 of the chili powder and cumin that I call for and take it up from there depending on taste.

Ingredients

1 medium red onion, chopped
1 green bell pepper, chopped
4 garlic cloves, chopped
1 tablespoon chili powder
1 tablespoon ground cumin
2 teaspoons unsweetened cocoa powder
1/4 teaspoon ground cinnamon
Kosher salt and black pepper
1 can (28 ounces) fire-roasted diced tomatoes
1 can (15-1/2 ounces) black beans, rinsed
1 can (15-1/2 ounces) kidney beans, rinsed
2 medium sweet potato (about 8 ounces), peeled and cut into 1/2-inch pieces
Sour cream, sliced scallions, sliced radishes, and tortilla chips, for serving

Directions

In a 4 to 6 quart slow cooker, combine the onion, bell pepper, garlic, chili powder, cumin, cocoa, cinnamon, 1 teaspoon salt, and 1/4 teaspoon black pepper.

Add the tomatoes (and their liquid), beans, sweet potato, and 1 cup water.

Cover and cook on LOW for 7 to 8 hours or for 4 to 5 hours on HIGH, or until the sweet potatoes are tender and the chili has thickened.

Serve the chili with the sour cream, scallions, radishes, and tortilla chips.

Nutritional Information (per serving)

Calories: 244; Total Fat: 2.0g; Cholesterol: 0mg; Sodium: 804mg; Carbohydrates: 45.6g; Dietary Fiber: 11.9g; Protein: 11.3g

Potatoes

THE RECIPES

Scalloped Potatoes

Cooking time: 3 to 4 hours (HIGH)
Serves 4

You can make these cheesy slow cooker scalloped potatoes dairy-free and vegan by substituting the regular cream cheese for a vegan cream cheese, such as Tofutti.

Ingredients

1/2 onion, diced
2 cloves garlic, minced
1 tablespoon parsley
1 teaspoon salt
Pepper to taste
7 to 8 potatoes, sliced thin
8 ounce cream cheese (use Tofutti if vegan)

Preparation

Lightly grease the slow cooker.

In a small bowl, combine the onion, garlic, parsley, salt, and pepper.

Place a layer of the sliced potatoes on the bottom of the slow cooker then sprinkle with some of the onion and garlic mixture. Top with 1/3 of the cream cheese. Continue layering the potatoes, spices and cream cheese. Sprinkle the top with additional salt and pepper.

Cover and cook on HIGH for 3 to 4 hours, or until the potatoes are done cooking.

Nutritional Information (per serving)

Calories: 463; Total Fat: 20.2g; Cholesterol: 62mg; Sodium: 773mg; Carbohydrates: 61.9g; Dietary Fiber: 9.2g; Protein: 10.8g

Sweet Potatoes

Cooking time: 4 to 5 hours (LOW)
Serves 4

Slow cooked sweet potatoes with apples and spices is a healthy vegetarian and vegan side dish that is perfect for Thanksgiving or any day. If your oven is full, make your sweet potatoes in the slow cooker instead.

Ingredients

4 to 5 sweet potatoes, sliced or chopped
2 apples, chopped
1/4 cup maple syrup
2 tablespoons brown sugar
2 tablespoons margarine, melted
1/4 teaspoon cinnamon
1/4 teaspoon nutmeg
Salt and pepper to taste

Preparation

Place the apples and sweet potatoes in a slow cooker.

Sprinkle the remaining ingredients on top of the potatoes and apples.

Cook on LOW for 4 to 5 hours.

Add more salt and pepper to taste.

These easy sweet potatoes are wheat-free and gluten-free.

Nutritional Information (per serving)

Calories: 324; Total Fat: 5.8g; Cholesterol: 0mg; Sodium: 110mg;
Carbohydrates: 69.5g; Dietary Fiber: 4.9g; Protein: 0.1g

Easy Potatoes with Cheese

Cooking time: 7 hours (LOW)
Serves 4

This is a simple slow cooker recipe for baked potatoes with Parmesan cheese. If you need a quick side dish, try these easy potatoes. All you need to do is chop them in the morning and they're ready to go by dinner.

Ingredients

4 to 5 potatoes, chopped
2 tablespoons margarine
1/2 onion, diced
1/2 teaspoon salt
1/4 teaspoon black pepper
1/4 cup freshly grated Parmesan cheese (optional)

Preparation

Sprinkle the salt and pepper over the potatoes in the slow cooker.

Spread the margarine on top and add the onion.

Cover and cook on LOW for 7 hours.

Sprinkle with cheese if desired.

Nutritional Information (per serving)

Calories: 230; Total Fat: 7.7g; Cholesterol: 6mg; Sodium: 466mg; Carbohydrates: 35.1g; Dietary Fiber: 5.4g; Protein: 6.2g

Slow Cooker Skillet Rosemary Potatoes

Cooking time: 3 to 4 hours (HIGH) or 6 to 8 hours (LOW)
Serves 4

This dish is two side dishes rolled into one (potatoes and carrots).

Ingredients

7 cups of quartered medium-sized red potatoes (about 8 potatoes), cut into wedges
1 sweet or yellow onion, coarsely cut into chunks
2 cups baby carrots
2 tablespoons olive oil
1 tablespoon finely chopped fresh rosemary, packed
1/2 teaspoon salt
1/2 teaspoon pepper

Preparation

In a large bowl, combine the potato wedges, onions, carrots, olive oil, rosemary, and salt and pepper until the vegetables are evenly coated with oil and the seasonings.

Coat the inside of the slow cooker with olive oil cooking spray.

Spoon the potato mixture inside, drizzling any oil or seasoning in the bottom of the bowl over the top.

Cook on HIGH for 3 to 4 hours or LOW for 6 to 8 hours.

Enjoy!

Nutritional Information (per serving)

Calories: 234; Total Fat: 7.3g; Cholesterol: 0mg; Sodium: 391mg;
Carbohydrates: 40.6g; Dietary Fiber: 6.2g; Protein: 5.1g

Hash Brown Casserole

Cooking time: 1-1/2 hours (HIGH), plus 2-1/2 hours (LOW)
Serves 8 to 10

The traditional hash brown casserole side dish has never been easier. You can prepare this recipe ahead of time and start cooking when you need to. This dish is also great to take to parties.

Ingredients

2 cups sour cream
1 can (10-3/4 ounces) cream of mushroom soup, condensed, undiluted
2 cups processed cheese, shredded
1/2 cup onion, chopped
1/4 teaspoon salt
1/4 teaspoon pepper
32 ounce potatoes (frozen hash brown, thawed)

Preparation

Stir together the sour cream, cream of mushroom soup, cheese, onion, salt and pepper in a large bowl.

Gradually mix in the hash browns until evenly coated.

Coat the inside of a slow cooker with cooking spray or butter.

Spoon the hash brown mixture into the slow cooker.

Cover, and cook on HIGH for 1-1/2 hours then reduce heat to LOW and cook for an additional 2-1/2 hours.

Nutritional Information (per serving)

Calories: 292; Total Fat:19g; Cholesterol: 43mg; Sodium: 626mg;
Carbohydrates: 22.8g; Dietary Fiber: 2.5g; Protein: 8.5g

Rice

THE RECIPES

Curried Rice and Lentils

Cooking time: 4 to 5 hours (LOW)
Serves 4

This recipe was inspired by the more traditional Indian recipes. Curried rice and lentils is a full vegetarian and vegan meal right out of your slow cooker. It couldn't be simpler.

Ingredients

1 cup rice
1 tablespoon curry powder
3-1/2 cups vegetable broth
1/2 cup lentils
2 vegetarian bouillon cubes
1/2 teaspoon garlic powder
1/4 teaspoon pepper
1 onion, diced

Preparation

Combine all the ingredients in a slow cooker.

Cover and cook on LOW for 4 to 5 hours.

Nutritional Information (per serving)

Calories: 309; Total Fat: 20g; Cholesterol: 0mg; Sodium: 979mg; Carbohydrates: 6.4g; Dietary Fiber: 9.0g; Protein: 14.6g

Easy Spanish Rice

Cooking time: 6 to 8 hours (LOW)
Serves 4

If you like Spanish rice, then you need to try this simple vegetarian Spanish rice recipe that you can make right in your slow cooker. Substituting the meat-based stock with vegetable broth or water makes this Spanish rice recipe both vegetarian and vegan. And using prepared and canned ingredients makes it easy to prepare.

Ingredients

2 cups rice
1 onion, diced
1 green bell pepper, diced
1 can (15 ounces) diced tomatoes, including liquid
1-3/4 cups water or vegetable broth
1-1/2 teaspoons garlic powder
2 teaspoons chili powder
1 teaspoon onion powder
1/4 cup salsa

Preparation

Combine all the ingredients in a slow cooker.

Cook on LOW for 6 to 8 hours.

Nutritional Information (per serving)

Calories: 391; Total Fat: 1.2g; Cholesterol: 0mg; Sodium: 127mg;
Carbohydrates: 85.5g; Dietary Fiber: 4.4g; Protein: 8.8g

Rice Vegetable Medley

Cooking time: 6 hours (HIGH) or 2 hours (LOW)
Serves 6

To have everything cooked the way it should, it is important that this slow cooker meal be layered in the order given. If the veggies are not from your garden, be sure to choose organic when possible.

Ingredients

1 large onion, sliced and peeled
2 cups uncooked white rice
2 sliced carrots (peeling optional)
1 cup sliced broccoli
1 cup fresh or frozen green beans
1 sliced green bell pepper with seeds and core discarded
1 sliced zucchini
1 cup corn kernels
1/2 cup sliced mushrooms
1 cup green peas

For the Sauce

2-1/2 cups tomato sauce
1/4 cup soy sauce with low sodium
2 tablespoons parsley
1/2 teaspoon cinnamon
1 teaspoon dry mustard
1 teaspoon ground thyme
2 teaspoons chili powder
1 teaspoon basil

Preparation

Layer the vegetables in a slow cooker in the order given in the ingredient list.

In a medium bowl, combine the tomato sauce and soy sauce. Stir well. Add the herbs and spices and mix it all together. Pour the sauce over the veggies in the slow cooker.

Cover the slow cooker and cook on HIGH for 6 hours or on LOW for 12 hours.

<u>Nutritional Information (per serving)</u>

Calories: 337;Total Fat: 1.4g; Cholesterol: 0mg; Sodium: 850mg; Carbohydrates: 72.4g; Dietary Fiber: 7.2g; Protein: 10.4g

Wild Rice with Cranberries

Cooking time: 4 to 5 hours (LOW), plus 15 minutes (LOW)
Serves 6

This is an easy way to cook wild rice and is perfect for Thanksgiving and Christmas!

Ingredients

1-1/2 cups uncooked wild rice
1 tablespoon butter, melted
1/2 teaspoon salt
1/4 teaspoon pepper
4 medium green onions, sliced, about 1/4 cup
2 cans (14 ounces, each) vegetable broth
1 can (4 ounces) sliced mushrooms, undrained
1/2 cup slivered almonds
1/3 cup dried cranberries or 1/3 cup dried cherries

Preparation

Mix all the ingredients, except the almonds and cranberries, in a slow cooker.

Cover and cook on LOW for 4 to 5 hours, or until the wild rice is tender.

Meanwhile, cook the almonds in an un-greased heavy skillet over MEDIUM-LOW heat for 5 to 7 minutes, stirring frequently until they start to brown, then stir constantly until golden brown. Set aside.

When the rice is tender, stir in the almonds and cranberries into the rice mixture in the slow cooker.

Cover and continue cooking on LOW for 15 minutes.

Nutritional Information (per serving)

Calories: 236; Total Fat: 7.1g; Cholesterol: 5mg; Sodium: 634mg; Carbohydrates: 34.2g; Dietary Fiber: 4.2g; Protein: 11.1g

Rice and Bean Stuffed Red Bell Peppers

Cooking time: 5 hours (LOW) or 3 hours (HIGH)
Serves 6

This is a delicious and very simple, make-ahead-of-time vegetarian meal!

Ingredients

6 red peppers
1 can (15 ounces) chili
1 cup cooked rice
1 cup shredded Monterey jack cheese
2 can (15 ounces, each) diced tomatoes, with green chilies
Low-fat sour cream (for serving)

Preparation

Remove the tops, membranes and seeds from the red peppers.

Stir together the rice, chili, and 1/2 of the cheese. Spoon the mixture into the peppers.

Pour the diced tomatoes and juice into a 5 to 6 quart slow cooker.

Placed the stuffed peppers filled side up into the slow cooker.

Cover and cook on LOW for 5 hours or HIGH for 3 hours.

Scoop out the peppers to a serving plate and spoon the tomato sauce from the bottom of the slow cooker over the peppers. Top with the remaining grated cheese.

Serve with sour cream.

Nutritional Information (per serving)

Calories: 298; Total Fat: 10.1g; Cholesterol: 32mg; Sodium: 1,030mg; Carbohydrates: 38.7g; Dietary Fiber: 3.6g; Protein: 12.1g

Desserts

THE RECIPES

Rice Pudding

Cooking time: 5 to 6 hours (HIGH)
Serves 8

This is a dairy-free and vegan rice pudding recipe made in the slow cooker. By keeping this recipe dairy-free and vegan, you can enjoy a low fat desert.

Everyone enjoys their rice pudding a little bit different. So don't be afraid to personalize this basic vegan recipe by adding cranberries, nutmeg, strawberries, or even coconut milk.

Ingredients

8 cups vanilla soy milk
1 cup rice (uncooked)
1 cup sugar
3 tablespoons margarine
Dash salt
1 teaspoon vanilla
1/2 cup raisins
1/2 teaspoon cinnamon

Preparation

Combine all the ingredients in a slow cooker.

Cook on HIGH for 5 to 6 hours.

Stir once every hour, until the desired consistency is reached.

Cooking time may vary, depending on your slow cooker.

Nutritional Information (per serving)

Calories: 358; Total Fat: 7.5g; Cholesterol: 0mg; Sodium: 161mg;
Carbohydrates: 64.9g; Dietary Fiber: 3.7g; Protein: 8.0g

Cherry Pie "Dump" Cake

Cooking time: 3 hours (LOW)
Serves 6

It could not get any simpler! A cherry pie slow cooker "dump" cake recipe made with just three ingredients. Just "dump" a few ingredients into your slow cooker and this easy vegan cake is ready to go!

Ingredients

1 can (20 ounces) cherry pie filling
1 box yellow cake mix
1/2 cup margarine, melted

Preparation

Dump the cherry pie filling in the slow cooker.

In a separate bowl, mix together the margarine and cake mix then dump the mixture over the pie filling.

Cover and cook on LOW for 3 hours.

Serve with ice cream or whipped cream if desired.

Nutritional Information (per serving)

Calories: 473; Total Fat: 19.0g; Cholesterol: 1mg; Sodium: 577mg; Carbohydrates: 72.9g; Dietary Fiber: 1.2g; Protein: 3.3g

Chocolate Peanut Butter Cake

Cooking time: 2 to 2-1/2 hours (HIGH)
Serves 6

I have prepared this recipe for my family and many of my friends and always receive five out of five stars. This soft and fudgy, chocolate and peanut buttery cake is a keeper! And it's dairy-free and completely vegan, too. Eat it warm and fresh out of the slow cooker. All you need is to top it with your favorite vegan ice cream!

Ingredients

1 cup flour
1/2 cup sugar + 3/4 cup
3 tablespoons cocoa powder + 1/4 cup
1-1/2 teaspoon baking powder
1/2 cup soy milk
2 tablespoons vegan margarine, melted
1 teaspoon vanilla
2 cups boiling water
1/2 cup peanut butter

Preparation

Combine the flour, 1/2 cup sugar, 3 tablespoons cocoa powder and baking powder in a large mixing bowl.

Whisk in the soy milk, vegan margarine and vanilla. Mix until smooth.

Pour into a lightly greased slow cooker.

Combine the 3/4 cup sugar and 1/4 cup cocoa.

In a separate bowl, combine the boiling water and peanut butter and whisk until smooth. Add to the cocoa and sugar mixture and mix until well combined. Pour over the batter in the slow cooker.

Cover and cook on HIGH for 2 to 2-1/2 hours, or until a knife inserted into the center comes out clean.

Nutritional Information (per serving)

Calories: 418; Total Fat: 15.6g; Cholesterol: 0mg; Sodium: 158mg;
Carbohydrates: 65.2g; Dietary Fiber: 2.9g; Protein: 8.8g

Chocolate Pudding Cake

Cooking time: 2-1/2 to 3 hours (HIGH)
Serves 8

If you're looking to try dessert recipes for your slow cooker, start with this easy, super yummy and moist chocolate pudding cake.

Ingredients

1 cup packed brown sugar
1 cup all-purpose flour
3 tablespoons unsweetened cocoa
2 teaspoons baking powder
1/2 teaspoon salt
1/2 cup milk
2 tablespoons butter, melted
1/2 teaspoon vanilla
1/4 cup unsweetened cocoa
3/4 cup packed brown sugar
1-3/4 cups boiling water

Preparation

Spray the slow cooker with baking spray.

Mix 1 cup brown sugar, flour, 3 tablespoons cocoa, baking powder and salt in a mixing bowl. Stir in the milk, butter and vanilla.

Spoon the batter into bottom of slow cooker (the dough will be very thick).

In another bowl, mix together the 3/4 cup brown sugar and 1/4 cup cocoa. Sprinkle evenly over the batter (Do not stir).

Pour boiling water over the top (Do not stir).

Cover and cook on HIGH for 2-1/2 to 3 hours or until the cake pulls away from the sides of the crock-pot (the pudding will be bubbling through).

Serve immediately with ice cream or whipped topping if desired. Or let set for 10 minutes and then invert onto a plate. Spoon the pudding left in the pot over the cake.

Nutritional Information (per serving)

Calories: 385; Total Fat: 4.0g; Cholesterol: 10mg; Sodium: 341mg; Carbohydrates: 62.0g; Dietary Fiber: 2.0g; Protein: 3.0g

Cranberry Peach Cobbler

Cooking time: 4 to 6 hours (LOW)
Serves 4

This slow cooker Cranberry Peach Cobbler makes for a sweet breakfast treat or a light dessert. The cranberries add texture and color, making for a vibrant and tasty recipe. You can serve your peach cobbler recipe plain or with a spoonful of whipped cream. This recipe is both vegetarian and vegan.

Ingredients

5 to 6 peaches, sliced
2 tablespoons flour
1/4 cup sugar
1/3 cup dried cranberries
1/4 teaspoon cinnamon
2/3 cup quick cooking oats
1 cup water
3 tablespoons melted margarine
3/4 cup brown sugar

Preparation

Toss the peaches in the flour and sugar in a large mixing bowl.

Add the cranberries, cinnamon and oats.

Place the water and peach mixture into the slow cooker.

Pour the margarine over the peaches and sprinkle with the brown sugar.

Cover and cook on LOW for 4 to 6 hours, or until the peaches are tender.

Nutritional Information (per serving)

Calories: 258; Total Fat: 9.5g; Cholesterol: 0mg; Sodium: 104mg;
Carbohydrates: 64.2g; Dietary Fiber: 3.8g; Protein: 3.4g

Conclusion

As you have seen in this cookbook, when it comes to creating tasty vegetarian meals in a slow cooker, the possibilities are endless. I encourage you to experiment and let you creative forces and imagination run wild and modify these recipes to your liking.

I sincerely hope that I have done a good job in introducing you to 30 of my favorite vegetarian slow cooker recipes and that I have provided valuable information that will help you in preparing your own fantastic vegetarian slow cooker meals.

If you enjoyed this cookbook, then you may also enjoy my other books:

- Pressure Cooker Recipe Book: Fast Cooking Under Extreme Pressure

- Slow Cooker International Cooking: A Culinary Journey of Set It & Forget It Meals

- 5 Ingredients 15 Minutes Prep Time Slow Cooker Cookbook: Quick & Easy Set It & Forget It Recipes

- 4 Ingredients or Less Cookbook: Fast, Practical & Healthy Meal Options

- Vegetarian Slow Cooker Recipes: Top 71 Quick & Easy Vegetarian Crockpot Recipe Book

- Vegetarian Pressure Cooker Recipe Book: 50 High Pressure Recipes for Busy People

- Gluten-Free Diet Cookbook: Healthier Eating Choices for People with Celiac Disease

- Satisfying Slower Cooker Meals and More

For more information about myself and to enjoy more amazing recipes, please follow these links:

- Maria Holmes author page at www.Amazon.com

- www.holmescookedmeals.com

- Holmes Cooked Meals Facebook page

I will be writing and publishing more cookbooks in the future, so please stay tuned. But for now, I would like to thank you for helping me and supporting my efforts to share my passion for cooking.

Thank you!

Index

CPSIA information can be obtained
at www.ICGtesting.com
Printed in the USA
LVHW041108120119
603692LV00023B/377

9 781494 477370